VITAL **TO EARTH!**
Keystone Species Explained

T0011440

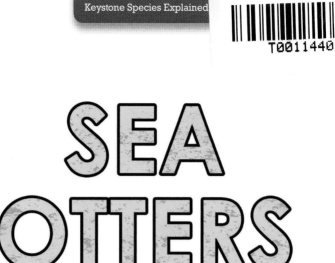

SEA OTTERS
IN THEIR ECOSYSTEMS

by Della O'Dowd

BEARPORT
PUBLISHING

Minneapolis, Minnesota

Credits
Cover and title page, © Michael S. Nolan/Alamy; 4–5, © Michael S. Nolan/Blue Planet Archive; 7, © Andrew b Stowe/Shutterstock; 8–9, © Erin Donalson/Getty; 10–11, © GomezDavid/iStock; 11, © Erin Donalson/Getty; 12–13, © anbusiello TW/Alamy; 14–15, © Alan Vernon/Getty; 17, © Cam/Adobe Stock; 18–19, © Internet Archive Book Images/Public Domain; 20–21, © Brent Durand/Getty; 22–23, © DurkTalsma/iStock; 24–25, © fdastudillo/iStock; 26–27, © Laura Hedien/Getty; 28, © jodyo.photos/Shutterstock; 29T, © PrathanChorruangsak/iStock; 29TM, © Wavebreakmedia/iStock; 29M, © ArtMarie/Stock; 29BM, © Ridofranz/iStock; 29B, © LeoPatrizi/iStock.

Bearport Publishing Company Product Development Team
President: Jen Jenson; Director of Product Development: Spencer Brinker; Managing Editor: Allison Juda; Associate Editor: Naomi Reich; Associate Editor: Tiana Tran; Art Director: Colin O'Dea; Designer: Elena Klinkner; Designer: Kayla Eggert; Product Development Assistant: Owen Hamlin

STATEMENT ON USAGE OF GENERATIVE ARTIFICIAL INTELLIGENCE
Bearport Publishing remains committed to publishing high-quality nonfiction books. Therefore, we restrict the use of generative AI to ensure accuracy of all text and visual components pertaining to a book's subject. See BearportPublishing.com for details.

Library of Congress Cataloging-in-Publication Data is available at www.loc.gov or upon request from the publisher.

ISBN: 979-8-88916-629-0 (hardcover)
ISBN: 979-8-88916-636-8 (paperback)
ISBN: 979-8-88916-642-9 (ebook)

For more information, write to Bearport Publishing, 5357 Penn Avenue South, Minneapolis, MN 55419.

Contents

Super Sea Otters

On a peaceful day in the **kelp** forest, fish swim between long, brown strands of seaweed swaying in the ocean current. Crabs scurry along on the sandy seafloor, darting between the growths. Along the surface of the water, a sea otter floats on its back, munching on a sea urchin snack.

Though it may look laid-back, the sea otter plays a major role in keeping life in the kelp forest healthy. These marine mammals are vital to the aquatic **ecosystems** where they live.

Sea otters are marine mammals. They have fur and give birth to live young. Though they must breathe air to survive, sea otters spend their whole lives in coastal waters near kelp forests.

A Friendly Forest

Kelp forests are some of the most **biodiverse** parts of the ocean. Growing in relatively shallow water, they are bursting with thousands of different kinds of life. These living things form a community to help one another survive.

The tall kelp plants slow down **tides** and waves. They create a still, peaceful place for underwater animals to make homes, raise their young, and stay safe from powerful storms. A complex food web keeps life below the waves well fed. Every living thing is connected.

Kelp are large, brown **algae** that grow in shallow waters close to the shore. Often, many strands of kelp grow close together, offering sea creatures lots of good spots to hide from **predators**.

Kelp can grow up to 2 feet (0.6 m) a day and reach heights of 200 ft (60 m)!

A Key Animal

Although sea otters are just some of the many members of kelp forest communities, they are essential. If sea otters were removed from these ecosystems, kelp forests would quickly disappear—and so would the life around them.

In their habitats, sea otters are a keystone **species**. That means they are crucial to supporting the entire community of life within an area. A keystone species shapes the land or helps balance the populations of plants and animals in a way that benefits everything in the ecosystem.

Sea otters live in groups. The furry creatures hold hands with one another and wrap themselves in kelp to keep from drifting away while eating and sleeping.

Sea otters gather in groups with up to 1,000 animals.

Staying Warm

The kelp forest has everything sea otters need to live in their cold ocean home. Unlike some marine mammals that beat the ocean's chill with a layer of fatty **blubber**, sea otters stay toasty with a combination of thick fur and by eating . . . a lot!

Their bodies turn food into energy and body heat. To stay warm, sea otters eat about a quarter of their body weight every day. They find this food in the kelp forest—a place often called nature's seafood buffet.

Otter fur is very thick. A single square inch (6.5 sq cm) of sea otter fur has ten times the amount of hair found on your entire head!

All You Can Eat!

While otters need a lot of food, they're not the only munchers. There's a whole lot of eating going on in a kelp forest! The kelp itself is food for many algae-eaters. Prawns, snails, crabs, jellyfish, sea stars, and sea urchins all eat the leafy forest. Then, otters, fish, and sea birds make meals out of these creatures, as well as the worms, maggots, and flies that live in the kelp. Sea lions, seals, and even larger birds feed on the fish.

Gray whales **graze** in kelp forests, sucking up tiny shellfish. They also rub up against the kelp to scrape their skin clean.

Sea lions hunt in forests, but they also hide their young from other predators among the tall kelp.

Cracking and Snacking

The kelp forest community stays well fed as long as the population stays balanced, with the right amount of creatures throughout the food web. This is where otters play a key role.

The biggest kelp-eaters—crabs, snails, sea urchins, clams, and mussels—have hard or spiky shells that keep most predators away. But otters have figured out how to get past these defenses. After catching their prey, the aquatic mammals float on their backs and place a rock on their furry bellies. They then smash the shelled creatures open on the rock. Dinner is served!

Otters have very sharp lower teeth for cutting meat. They also have little pouches of loose skin under their arms used for storing their shell-cracking rocks.

Too Much Munching

Lots of creatures munch on kelp, and most don't eat too much of the plants. However, sea urchins are different. If left unchecked, these spiny creatures can quickly take over—and take out—an entire kelp forest.

Sea urchins **reproduce** quickly. Their numbers grow out of hand if the animals don't face population control from hungry predators. They can soon overrun a whole forest and eat it up. Before long, the kelp forest that fed and housed thousands of species is gone.

Groups of sea urchins can eat 30 ft (9 m) of kelp a month. Once all the kelp is gone, these urchins can survive for years without a meal, even as the rest of life in the forest suffers.

Sea Otters in Danger

Thankfully, sea otters eat a lot of urchins. This helps keep life balanced in a kelp forest. However, sea otters have long been at risk themselves.

The sea otter population once stretched across the Pacific coastlines of northern Japan and down the Pacific Coast of California all the way to Mexico. Then, starting in the mid-1700s, people began hunting these animals for their thick, warm fur. Sea otters were pushed to the brink of **extinction** by the early 1900s.

Russian hunters were the first to kill sea otters for their fur. But by the height of the fur trade, hunters across Japan, Spain, England, and the United States were also killing the animals.

Sea otter fur was often made into clothing.

Suffering Forests

By 1911, there were only 13 groups of sea otters left in the world, each with fewer than 100 animals. The consequences soon spread throughout kelp forests. Without otters, uncontrollable sea urchins had no predators to keep their numbers down. Urchins chewed through the **holdfasts** on kelp that keep the plants attached to the seafloor. Cutting the kelp loose in this way kills it. Soon, forests disappeared, and the complex web of creatures that relied on these ecosystems for food and shelter went with them.

Kelp can take in **carbon**. This heat-trapping gas in our air causes **climate change**. Losing kelp forests means we risk speeding this up.

Bring the Otters Back

Once people noticed the problems that came after the otters disappeared, they took action. A law called the **International** Fur Seal Treaty made it illegal to hunt sea otters in international waters. However, as otters are coastal creatures, the real impact came when local governments banned hunting in waters near shore. In 1913, California made sea otters protected under state law. Slowly, the otter population began to grow again.

In 1938, a new group of about 50 otters was found off the coast of Central California. In the decades since, sea otter numbers have mostly increased. The population has swelled to 3,200 individuals.

The U.S. Marine Mammal Protection Act and the Endangered Species Act also helped sea otters. These laws kept the creatures safe and their ocean homes protected.

Forests Return

As sea otters came back into the ecosystems, kelp forests began to bounce back, too. With hungry otters on the scene, the number of sea urchins decreased quickly.

Those urchins that were not eaten by otters often hid to protect themselves. Instead of chewing through the holdfasts of kelp plants, they instead began eating only the stray pieces of kelp that floated down to the seafloor. Kelp forests began to grow again, and the animals of the kelp community returned shortly after, laying eggs, raising young, making meals, and settling down in their kelp forest homes.

Since scientists first learned about how otters help kelp forests, they have started using the key animals to bring ocean life back. They are **reintroducing** otters in places where they once lived along the Pacific Coast, from Northern California to Alaska.

Protecting Our Protectors

Although their populations are growing, sea otters still face many challenges. Pollution, chemicals, and other forms of waste washing into their watery homes make the otters sick. Continued protections are needed to keep these important predators safe and their entire ecosystems healthy.

Without sea otters, kelp forests would shrink with too many munching sea urchins. The furry animals maintain an important balance that keeps all the other species in the kelp forest healthy. Sea otters truly are key!

Oil spills are a major threat to sea otters and can harm many of them very quickly. Oil ruins the part of the otters' fur that keeps them warm, putting the creatures at risk of dying from the cold.

Save the Sea Otters

When sea otters suffer, kelp forests and all the life they support suffer, too. What can we do to help sea otters as they work to keep their ecosystems healthy?

Learn more about sea otters so you can let other people know how the animals are a keystone species.

Keep pollution out of the ocean. Do not pour any chemicals down your drain or into your gutters. What goes down your drain often ends up in the water.

Never litter, and join coastline cleanup days.

Write letters to companies and politicians explaining why it's important to prevent pollution and oil spills.

Join, donate to, or volunteer for sea otter protection programs.

Glossary

algae plantlike living things often found in water

biodiverse full of many different kinds of plants and animals

blubber a layer of fat under the skin of some animals, including seals, whales, and polar bears

carbon an element found in all plants and animals that can contribute to climate change

climate change changes in the usual weather around Earth, including the warming of the air and oceans, due to human activities

ecosystems communities of animals and plants that depend on one another to live

extinction when a type of plant or animal dies out completely

graze to eat plants

holdfasts the rootlike parts that aquatic plants use to cling to things

international having to do with countries around the world

kelp a type of seaweed that grows in long green or brown strips

predators animals that hunt and eat other animals

reintroducing bringing animals back into an area where they once lived

reproduce to have babies to make more of a living thing

species groups that plants and animals are divided into, according to similar characteristics

tides movement of water toward or away from the shore of an ocean or other large body of water

Read More

Bergin, Raymond. *Ocean Life Connections (Life on Earth! Biodiversity Explained).* Minneapolis: Bearport Publishing Company, 2023.

Cooke, Tim. *Fur-tastrophe Avoided: Southern Sea Otter Comeback (Saving Animals from the Brink).* Minneapolis: Bearport Publishing, 2022.

Griffin, Mary. *Kelp Forests (Fantastic Plants).* New York: PowerKids Press, 2023.

Learn More Online

1. Go to **www.factsurfer.com** or scan the QR code below.

2. Enter "**Keystone Sea Otters**" into the search box.

3. Click on the cover of this book to see a list of websites.

Index

About the Author

Della O'Dowd is a writer with a passion for nature. When she's not writing, she's hiking, drawing, or going on an adventure with her dog. It's her dream to visit every national park someday.